W9-AMQ-626

Wheels and Axles in Action

Gillian Gosman

PowerKiDS
press

New York

Published in 2011 by The Rosen Publishing Group, Inc.
29 East 21st Street, New York, NY 10010

First Edition

Editor: Maggie Murphy
Book Design: Kate Laczynski
Photo Researcher: Jessica Gerweck

Photo Credits: Cover, pp. 4, 5 (bottom), 14, 19 Shutterstock.com; p. 5 (top) Keren Su/Getty Images; back cover and interior cement background graphic © www.iStockphoto.com/walrusmail; back cover and interior graphic (behind some images) © www.iStockphoto.com/Ivan Gusev; p. 7 © Plus Pix/age fotostock; p. 8 © www.iStockphoto.com/Cenk Ertekin; p. 9 © Don Hammond/age fotostock; pp. 10–11 © www.iStockphoto.com/silverlining56; pp. 12, 16 SSPL/Getty Images; p. 13 Todd Klassy/Getty Images; p. 17 Three Lions/Getty Images; p. 18 Sean Justice/Getty Images; pp. 20–21 © Rosen Publishing; p. 22 Wolfgang Von Brauchitsch/Bloomberg/Getty Images.

Library of Congress Cataloging-in-Publication Data

Gosman, Gillian.
  Wheels and axles in action / Gillian Gosman. — 1st ed.
      p. cm. — (Simple machines at work)
  Includes index.
  ISBN 978-1-4488-0684-3 (library binding) — ISBN 978-1-4488-1301-8 (pbk.) — ISBN 978-1-4488-1302-5 (6-pack)
  1. Wheels—Juvenile literature. 2. Axles—Juvenile literature. I. Title.
  TJ181.5.G675 2011
  621.8—dc22

                                                    2010003771

Manufactured in the United States of America

CPSIA Compliance Information: Batch #WS10PK: For Further Information contact Rosen Publishing, New York, New York at 1-800-237-9932

Contents

What Is a Wheel and Axle?

The axle of a Ferris wheel is a rod that runs through the center of the wheel. Powerful engines turn this wheel and axle.

Have you ever ridden on a Ferris wheel, turned a doorknob, or watched an adult use a steering wheel in a car or truck? If so, you have seen a wheel and axle at work. A wheel and axle is a simple machine. Simple machines are ones with few moving parts. Besides the wheel and axle, there are five other

This well uses a wheel and axle to raise and lower a pail of water. When you turn the handle of this wheel, the handle makes the shape of a larger wheel around the smaller axle.

simple machines. They are the **inclined** plane, the **lever**, the screw, the wedge, and the pulley. Simple machines are often used together to make compound machines. Compound machines, also called **complex** machines, have many moving parts and are built to do certain jobs. A car, a dishwasher, and a lawn mower are all compound machines.

A steering wheel is a wheel and axle that helps guide the direction in which the wheels of a car are turned.

The Parts of a Wheel and Axle

AXLE

WHEEL

The simple machine called a wheel and axle is made up of two connected, circular parts of different sizes. The larger part is called a wheel and the smaller part is a rod called an axle. A wheel that turns around an axle but is not connected to the

6

axle is not the simple machine called a wheel and axle.

Some wheels and axles may have a wheel on just one end of the axle. Others may have wheels on both ends of the axle. Some wheels and axles are powered by human **effort**, such as a screwdriver. Others use engine power, such as a car, school bus, or truck.

When one part of the wheel and axle turns, the other part turns as well because the wheel is attached to the axle.

Some wheels, called gears, have teeth around their outer rims. These teeth join to other gears to do many different jobs.

A lever, such as a seesaw, makes it easy to lift a load that sits at one end of the plank. You simply apply force to the other end.

A wheel is really a kind of lever. Generally, a lever is a long **plank** that rests across a fixed point, called the **fulcrum**.

In the case of a wheel and axle, the wheel acts as one end of the lever and the axle acts as the other. The point at the center of both the wheel and the axle is the fulcrum. If you apply **force** to the wheel, the wheel multiplies your effort to make the **output** force of the axle greater. This is because the wheel is a larger circle than the axle. If you apply force to the axle, the wheel will turn a greater distance than the axle using only the effort it takes to turn the axle. This is because the axle is a smaller circle than the wheel.

In some parts of the world, this kind of wheel and axle is used to grind grain. When the girl turns the small handle of the axle, the big stone wheel turns as well and grinds the grain into powder.

A doorknob is one kind of wheel and axle. The circular knob is attached to an axle inside the door. This is used to turn the parts of the lock that open the door. You apply effort to the outside of the wheel when your hand turns the knob. The effort applied to turn the knob turns the axle as well because the wheel and axle are attached to each other.

Cars also use wheels and axles, but in cars, the axle itself spins from the power of the engine. When the axle

A doorknob is easy to use because the knob is a bigger circle than the axle. This makes it easier to turn than the smaller axle.

spins, the car's wheels also spin. The road offers resistance to the wheel's forward movement. However, the engine that powers the car makes an even greater effort, and the axle makes the wheels spin quickly.

The First Wheel and Axle

Potter's wheels were not used only in ancient times. Here, a man is shown using a potter's wheel in Great Britain at the beginning of the nineteenth century.

The first wheels were made by the people of **Mesopotamia** over 7,000 years ago. These wheels were made of solid stone or circles of wood cut from trees.

The earliest wheel and axle machines were used as **potter's wheels**. A potter's wheel is a flat, round stone. By applying effort to a pedal, the potter makes the stone spin on its axle. The potter works a piece of clay between her hands on the spinning stone, shaping the clay into a pot. Clay pots were very important in everyday life in ancient times. They were used to store food, water, and medicines.

Today, making pottery is a popular hobby. Some people even consider it a form of art!

Wheels and Axles Through Time

For thousands of years, wheels and axles were used to spin pots, to catch the power of water, to **grind** grain into flour, and even in ancient toys. Some people think that the wheel and axle could be one of the most important **inventions** of all time.

Early windmills used several wheels and axles to work. The large sails of a windmill turned on an axle by the power of the wind. The axle was joined to wheels and gears

The earliest windmills were built in present-day Iran, in about 250 BC. This is a windmill in the Netherlands, which is famous for its windmills.

within the mill building. They turned as the sails turned. These wheels carried the power of the wind to the **millstone**, which broke down corn or other grains into flour. Wheels and axles were also used to lift water from wells. These wheel and axle machines were called watermills.

Let's Travel by Wheel and Axle!

Here, an ancient Roman man loads barrels on the back of a wagon pulled by two horses.

Today when we think of wheels, we generally think of the vehicles that travel on the road. However, the use of the wheel as the best way to travel did not catch on quickly. First, people needed to train animals to pull wheeled wagons. Then they needed to build roads that were smooth enough and long enough to be useful.

In time, **wheelwrights** learned that the wheels would be lighter and faster if they were not solid. They cut long rods called spokes and used them to join the center of the wheel to its outer rim. Later, engines were used to power automobiles, which used wheels and axles for steering and to make the vehicle move quickly.

This photograph shows an early American automobile, the Model T, in 1924. The Model T was made by the Ford Motor Company from 1908 until 1927.

Wheels, Axles, and You

Some sinks have faucets with handles that look like levers. Others, such as this sink, have round handles that look more like wheels. Both kinds of handles work like wheels and axles.

You likely use many wheels and axles in your everyday life. The handles of the faucet on your bathroom sink work like a wheel and axle. When you turn the handle of the faucet in a circle, it turns the axle to which it is attached. The axle then opens and closes the pipes that allow water to flow out of the faucet.

A screwdriver uses the mechanical advantage of the axle to twist a screw into or out of place more easily than you could using just your fingers. When your hand grips the handle of a screwdriver and turns it, the axle turns as well and twists the screw into or out of place.

The handle of the screwdriver is the wheel, and the long metal piece that fits into the head of a screw is the axle.

step 2

On a wheel and axle, when you turn either the wheel or the axle, the other part turns as well. When you apply force to the wheel, the force of the axle is multiplied. It takes less effort for you to turn the wheel than the axle in order to get the job done. However, it takes more turns of the axle and a longer amount of time to get the job done than if you just turned the axle. This simple **experiment** will show you how this works.

What You Will Need:
- a hammer
- a screwdriver
- a nail
- a screw
- a piece of wood

1. Have an adult hammer a nail just a little bit into the piece of wood to make a starter hole for the screw.

2. Now, holding the long metal piece on the screwdriver instead of the handle, twist the screw into the wood.

3. When you are done, hammer another starter hole in the wood with a nail.

4. This time, hold the handle of the screwdriver and twist the screw into the wood. Was it easier to twist the screw into the wood holding the metal part of the screwdriver or the handle? Was it faster to twist the screw into the wood holding the metal part or the handle?

step 4

Wheels and Axles That Go Super Fast

Today, cars, buses, and trucks are everywhere. The jet engine of an airplane and the propeller of a helicopter also use wheels and axles. The steering wheel of a car or truck is a wheel and axle, too!

These compound machines are getting faster every year. Today, some cars, such as the Bugatti Veyron, can go more than 250 miles per hour (402 km/h)! This car is light and low to the ground and has a powerful engine. However, it is the wheel and axle that makes the movement of the car possible, carrying people very quickly!

Glossary

complex (kom-PLEKS) Having many parts.

effort (EH-fert) The amount of force applied to an object.

experiment (ik-SPER-uh-ment) A set of actions or steps taken to learn more about something.

force (FORS) Something that moves or pushes on something else.

fulcrum (FUL-krum) The point on which a lever moves.

grind (GRYND) To crush into tiny pieces.

inclined (in-KLYND) Having a slope.

inventions (in-VENT-shunz) New things made by people.

lever (LEH-vur) A rod that moves at a fixed point.

Mesopotamia (mes-uh-puh-TAY-mee-uh) The ancient name for the land between the Tigris and Euphrates rivers.

millstone (MIL-stohn) A heavy, circular stone used for making grain into a powder.

output (OWT-puht) Something produced by an action.

plank (PLANGK) A long, flat piece of wood or metal.

potter's wheels (PAH-terz WEELZ) Tablelike disks that spin and are used to make pottery.

wheelwrights (WEEL-ryts) People who make and repair wheels.

Index

Web Sites

Due to the changing nature of Internet links, PowerKids Press has developed an online list of Web sites related to the subject of this book. This site is updated regularly. Please use this link to access the list:

www.powerkidslinks.com/sm/wheel/